A Day in the Life: Desert Animals

Bactrian Camel

Anita Ganeri

www.raintreepublishers.co.uk
Visit our website to find out more information about Raintree books.

To order:
☎ Phone 0845 6044371
🖷 Fax +44 (0) 1865 312263
✉ Email myorders@raintreepublishers.co.uk

Customers from outside the UK please telephone +44 1865 312262

Raintree is an imprint of Capstone Global Library Limited, a company incorporated in England and Wales having its registered office at 7 Pilgrim Street, London, EC4V 6LB – Registered company number: 6695582

Text © Capstone Global Library Limited 2011
First published in hardback in 2011
First published in paperback in 2012
The moral rights of the proprietor have been asserted.

Edited by Daniel Nunn, Rebecca Rissman, and Sian Smith
Designed by Richard Parker
Picture research by Elizabeth Alexander
Production by Victoria Fitzgerald
Originated by Capstone Global Library Ltd
Printed and bound in China by South China Printing Company Ltd

ISBN 978 1 406 21960 9 (hardback)
14 13 12 11 10
10 9 8 7 6 5 4 3 2 1

ISBN 978 1 406 22123 7 (paperback)
15 14 13 12
10 9 8 7 6 5 4 3 2 1

British Library Cataloguing in Publication Data

Ganeri, Anita, 1961-
  Bactrian camel. -- (A day in the life. Desert animals)
  1. Bactrian camel--Juvenile literature.
  I. Title II. Series
  599.6'362-dc22

Acknowledgements

We would like to thank the following for permission to reproduce photographs: Alamy p. 18 (© Vic Pigula), Corbis pp. 4 (© Tuul/Hemis), 5, 23 glossary desert, 23 glossary dromedary (© photocake.de/plainpicture), 14 (© Guo Jian She/Redlink), 20 (© Frans Lanting); FLPA pp. 10, 23 glossary herd (ImageBroker), 11 (Colin Monteath/ Minden Pictures); Getty Images pp. 15 (Peter DeMarco), 17, 23 glossary mammal (Art Wolfe/The Image Bank); iStockphoto pp. 12, 23 glossary energy (© Anna Yu), 22, 23 glossary hump (© David Kerkhoff), 23 glossary fat (© Jolanta Dabrowska); Photolibrary pp. 8 (Bruno Morandi/ age fotostock), 9, 23 glossary nostrils (Juniors Bildarchiv), 16 (Konstantin Mikhailov/Russian Look), 19 (Guido Alberto Rossi/Tips Italia), 21 (E.R. DEGGINGER/Animals Animals); Shutterstock pp. 7, 13 (© Pichugin Dmitry). Front cover photograph of a Bactrian camel reproduced with permission of Corbis © Theo Allofs.

Back cover photograph of (left) a Bactrian camel eating (Camelus bactrianus domesticus) reproduced with permission of iStockphoto (© Anna Yu); and (right) a Bactrian camel in the Mongolian Desert reproduced with permission of Shutterstock (© Pichugin Dmitry).

We would like to thank Michael Bright for his assistance in the preparation of this book.

Every effort has been made to contact copyright holders of material reproduced in this book. Any omissions will be rectified in subsequent printings if notice is given to the publisher.

Contents

Some words are shown in bold, **like this**.
You can find them in the glossary on page 23.

What is a Bactrian camel?

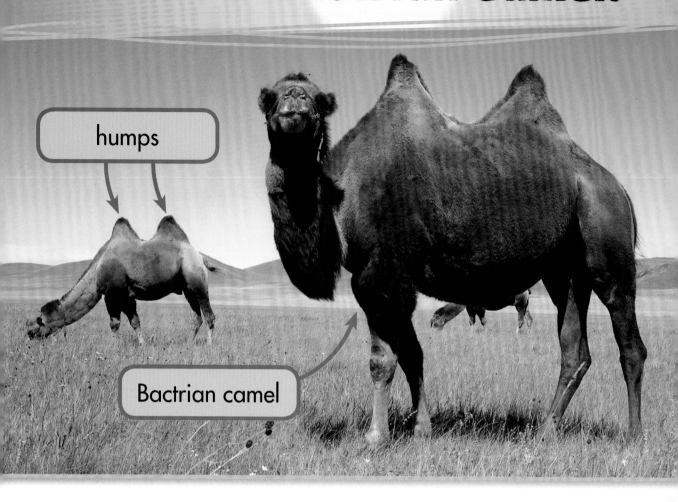

humps

Bactrian camel

A camel is a **mammal**.

All mammals have some hair on their bodies and feed their babies milk.

hump

dromedary

Camels which only have one **hump** are called **dromedaries**.

This book is about Bactrian camels that have two humps.

Where do Bactrian camels live?

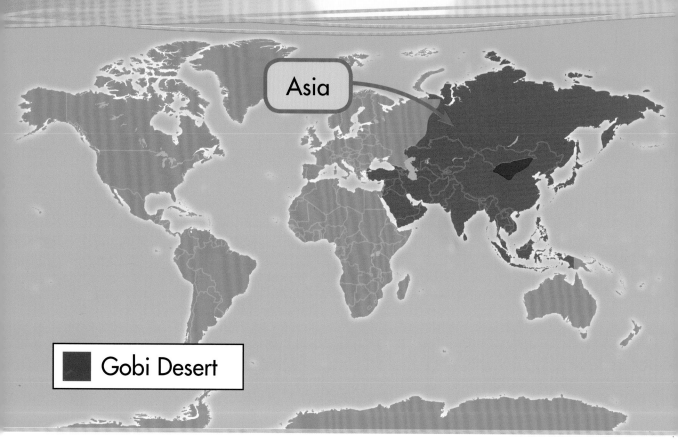

Asia

Gobi Desert

Bactrian camels live in the Gobi **Desert** in Asia.

Can you find this desert on the map?

The desert is hot in the summer but cold in winter, with very little rain.

Most of the desert is rocky and stony, with some sand.

What do Bactrian camels look like?

coat

Bactrian camels are large, with long necks, long legs, and two big **humps**.

Their brown coats grow thicker in winter to keep them warm.

eyelashes

nostril

A Bactrian camel has thick eyelashes for keeping dust and sand out of its eyes.

It can also close its **nostrils** to stop sand and dust from getting in.

What do Bactrian camels do in the day?

Bactrian camels look for food in the morning.

They walk long distances to find food and water.

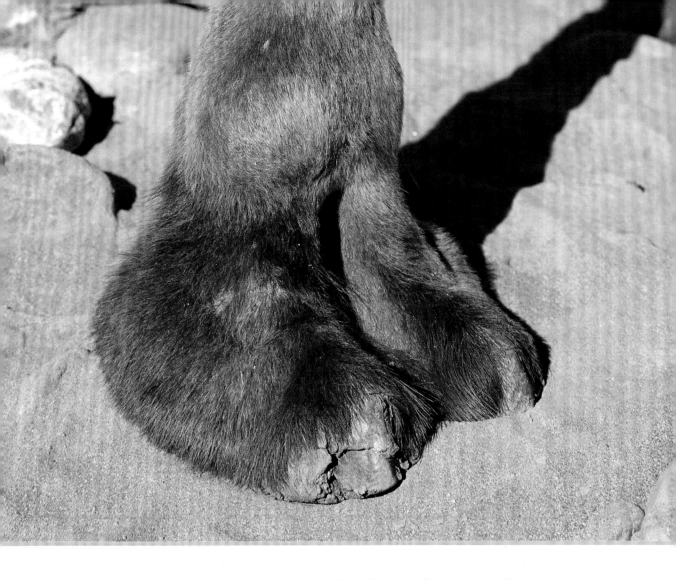

The camels have tough feet for walking on rocky ground.

They can also spread their toes out wide for walking on soft, sandy ground.

What do Bactrian camels eat?

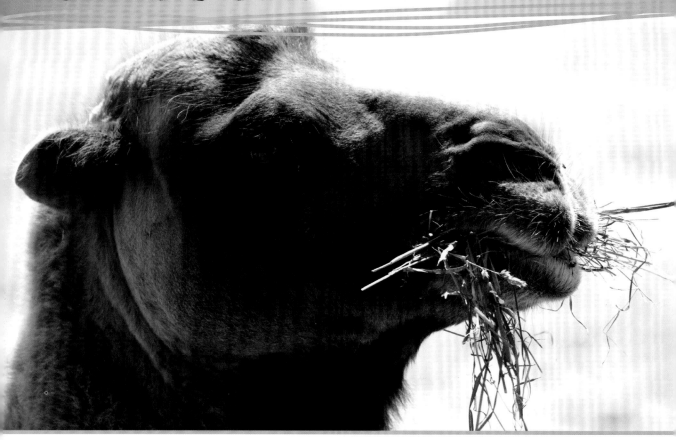

Bactrian camels mostly eat **desert** plants they find in the day.

They have tough mouths and can even eat prickly or thorny plants.

A camel's **hump** is a store of **fat**.

The camels use the fat to give them **energy** when they cannot find food to eat.

Do Bactrian camels need to drink?

Bactrian camels can go for days without drinking water.

This is useful in the **desert** where there is not much water.

If the camels find some water, they can drink about six bucketfuls in one go.

They also get water from the plants they eat.

Do Bactrian camels live in groups?

Bactrian camels live in family groups, called **herds**.

There are usually about six camels in a herd, but sometimes more.

Baby camels are born in spring.

A baby stays in the herd with its mother until it is about three years old.

Do Bactrian camels have any enemies?

People have hunted wild Bactrian camels for a long time.

There are not many wild Bactrian camels left.

Some people use Bactrian camels and keep them safe.

Bactrian camels can help people to carry things across the **desert**.

What do Bactrian camels do at night?

At night, the camels go to sleep on the ground.

Their thick fur keeps them warm.

The camels sleep with their legs tucked under their bodies.

They hold their heads high up in the air.

Bactrian camel body map

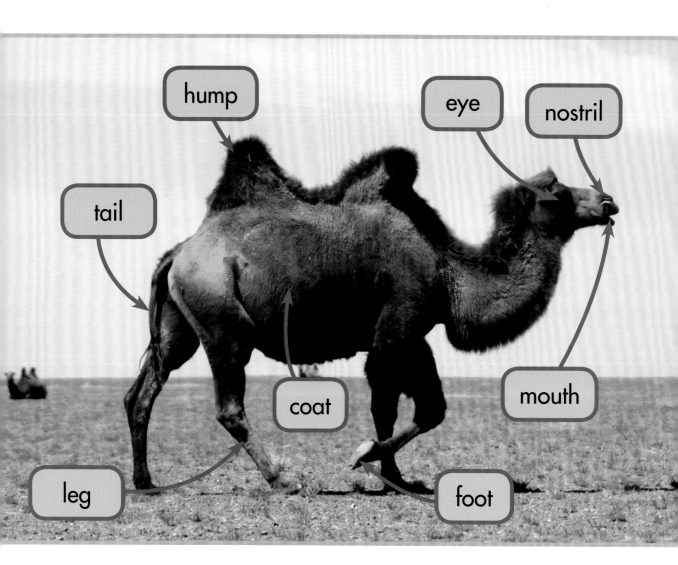

hump

eye

nostril

tail

coat

mouth

leg

foot

Glossary

 **desert** very dry place that is rocky, stony, or sandy

 **dromedary** camel with one hump

 **energy** power to do something

 **fat** oily thing in some foods. Animals use fat in their bodies to give them energy.

 **herd** family group of camels

 **hump** store of fat on a camel's back

 **mammal** animal that feeds its babies milk. All mammals have some hair or fur on their bodies.

 **nostrils** openings around a camel's nose

Find out more

Books

Desert Animals (Focus on Habitats), Stephen Savage (Wayland, 2006)

Deserts (My World of Geography), Angela Royston (Heinemann Library, 2004)

24 Hours: Desert (Focus on Habitats), Elizabeth Haldane (Dorling Kindersley, 2006)

Websites

Learn more about Bactrian camels at:
kids.nationalgeographic.com/kids/animals/creaturefeature/camels

Look at lots of videos and pictures of Bactrian camels at:
www.arkive.org/wild-bactrian-camel/camelus-ferus/

Index